the Alphabet Zoo

Guess Who's Hiding at

the Alphabet Zoo?

ALL RIGHTS RESERVED

the Alphabet Zoo

Author and Cover artwork:

Don Ford

Publisher's Note:

This is a work of non- fiction.

Many of these friends are actually considered endangered species. My hope in creating this book is to raise awareness of the needs of animals across the globe. Let's all care!

Fine Design Publishing, Don Ford ©2013

Dedication:

This book is dedicated to anyone who loves animals and cares for them!

Who's hiding at the Alphabet Zoo?

A: "Please don't eat me",
Said the little ant .

This first one should be easy

You now know what I eat

My nose is like a vacuum hose

I suck them off their feet

Who am I? Learn about me.

See animal glossary at the end

3

Who's hiding at the Alphabet Zoo?

B: My favorite food is Honey!

Sometimes I climb up trees

My fur is black or brown

I climb to get the honey

I eat it and I climb back down

Who am I? Learn about me.

See animal glossary at the end

4

Who's hiding at the Alphabet Zoo?

C: I carry lots of water.

Across the hottest desert

My back one hump or two

I carry all the water

And I carry even you.

Who am I? Learn about me.

See animal glossary at the end

Who's hiding at the Alphabet Zoo?

D: Some go south in Winter

Unlike some other birds
I make funny quacking sounds
I flap my wings I have web feet
in ponds I Just swim around

Who am I? Learn about me.

See animal glossary at the end

Who's hiding at the Alphabet Zoo?

E: A mouse can really Scare me !

I'm very big and weigh a lot

I have these giant ears

My trunk it sprays out water

My size is greatly feared.

Who am I? Learn about me.

See animal glossary at the end

7

Who's hiding at the Alphabet Zoo?

F: I have a bushy Red tail.

I'm sneaky and I'm sly
I have red fur all over
I always try to trick you
I can lay low in the clover.

Who am I? Learn about me.

See animal glossary at the end

Who's hiding at the Alphabet Zoo?

G: I eat leaves at the top of trees.

Way up high in the sky

Just like a gentle giant stands

The longest neck of all have I

I gallop fast on the land.

Who am I? Learn about me.

See animal glossary at the end

9

Who's hiding at the Alphabet Zoo?

H: three letter ps are in my name

Into the water you see me go

I have a great big mouth &teeth

I always love to take a swim

Don't get close, stay clear of me

Who am I? Learn about me.

See animal glossary at the end

10

Who's hiding at the Alphabet Zoo?

I: I am lizard like.

You can call me lizard
Or you can call me Lizzy
I slowly crawl along the sand
Moving fast makes me dizzy.

Who am I? Learn about me.

See animal glossary at the end

11

Who's hiding at the Alphabet Zoo?

J: I am a big, big wild cat

I run real fast across the plain
For a big cat I can move
They've clocked me going 35
Miles an hour – it is true.

Who am I? Learn about me.

See animal glossary at the end

12

Who's hiding at the Alphabet Zoo?

K: I have a pouch and jump real high

I am a mother with a baby

Tucked in the front of me

It's deep inside a pocket

Safe and warm as it can be.

Who am I? Learn about me.

See animal glossary at the end

13

Who's hiding at the Alphabet Zoo?

L: lamb is in my name.

I may look funny head held high

My wool is soft as a lamb's

My coat could make a sweater

I'm proud of who I am.

Who am I? Learn about me.

See animal glossary at the end

14

Who's hiding at the Alphabet Zoo?

M: I am a real Swinger.

From branch to vine in trees

I get around quite easily

I hang by hands & feet & tail

A ripe banana pleases me.

Who am I? Learn about me.

See animal glossary at the end

15

Who's hiding at the Alphabet Zoo?

N: I am the upside–

down Bird.

I could be an acrobat

I hang all upside down

I can walk on ceilings

Or just fly all around.

Who am I? Learn about me.

See animal glossary at the end

Who's hiding at the Alphabet Zoo?

O: I have more arms than you – 8 in all

My arms are full of suction cups

And stick to anything around

I live deep in the ocean

Where many fish abound.

Who am I? Learn about me.

See animal glossary at the end

17

Who's hiding at the Alphabet Zoo?

P: I'm cool in my tuxedo.

Most of what I eat is fish
So toss me one right now
I live up north in all the cold
I manage to stay warm somehow.

Who am I? Learn about me.

See animal glossary at the end

18

Who's hiding at the Alphabet Zoo?

Q: i'm a bird with a funny
thing on my head

I'm quite the bird to see

My tail is like a fan

I live deep in the woods

Away from one called man.

Who am I? Learn about me.

See animal glossary at the end

19

Who's hiding at the Alphabet Zoo?

R: on my nose is one big horn and one small one.

Watch me when I'm charging

I'm very fast they say

And if you make me mad

You better run away.

Who am I? Learn about me.

See animal glossary at the end

20

Who's hiding at the Alphabet Zoo?

S: I can bounce balls on my nose

I swim in the ocean
I can walk on the ice
I eat fish all day
They are tasty and nice

Who am I? Learn about me.

See animal glossary at the end

21

Who's hiding at the Alphabet Zoo?

T: I am a big striped cat.

You know me by colors

Of black and of orange

The country of India

Is where I was born.

Who am I? Learn about me.

See animal glossary at the end

22

Who's hiding at the Alphabet Zoo?

U: I was a legend in my own time.

I am not real but make believe

I gallop over all the land

I'm told about in fairytales

A horn upon my forehead stands

Who am I? Learn about me.

See animal glossary at the end

23

Who's hiding at the Alphabet Zoo?

V: Sometimes I'm called a flying mouse.

I'm not as scary as my name

My radar is quite keen

At night is when I fly around

black or brown and seldom seen.

Who am I? Learn about me.

See animal glossary at the end

24

Who's hiding at the Alphabet Zoo?

W: the world's largest mammal

The biggest fish that's me

My fat they call it blubber

I give my babies milk

We are the greatest mothers

Who am I? Learn about me.

See animal glossary at the end

25

Who's hiding at the Alphabet Zoo?

X: In water you see right through me.

My other name is tetra fish

All the colors of the rainbow

I have a glass-like body

In fish tanks I put on a show

Who am I? Learn about me.

See animal glossary at the end

26

Who's hiding at the Alphabet Zoo?

Y: I look like a cross between a cow and a small buffalo.

I have two horns upon my head

And eat grass just the same

Black or brown with shaggy HAIR

Born wild – I can't be tamed.

Who am I? Learn about me.

See animal glossary at the end

27

Who's hiding at the Alphabet Zoo?

Z: I am a big striped horse.

You know me by my colors

Simple black and white

I gallop very fast they say

If lions come, I'm out of sight.

Who am I? Learn about me.

See animal glossary at the end

28

A is for Anteater:

I live throughout South and Central America. My main diet consists of ants and termites. My tongue is more than 2 feet long and it works well to get into cavities and tunnels built by various insects. I am not dangerous to man, but some folks think because I can grow to four foot long that I am big and scary.

B is for Bear:

I am not one to toy with, especially when I am with my young. I am very protective of them. Never attempt to feed me. We all have our bad days. Most of the other animals in the woods stay clear of me and you should also. The sign says do not feed the bears.

C is for Camel:

I can cross the hottest dessert, because I can carry up to 990 pounds of water. Even with my two humps on my back, I like how I look.

D is for Duck:

Though ponds are my favorite place to land and swim, I also fly to lakes and streams. The sound of quacking I make is unlike any other animal. Our eggs are nearly twice the size of a regular chicken's egg.

30

E is for Elephant:

I am the largest land animal and live mostly in Africa. You can't miss hearing us when we run; the ground will shake under your feet when we come near. So stay clear of our herds as we come thundering through.

F is for Fox:

Though red is our normal color, a few of us are gray but are called silver foxes. They always call us sly, but we are really just keen of sight which makes us very observant. We live in holes in trees and caves, called dens. We live right here in America. We are also found throughout all of Europe and even in Australia.

is for Giraffe:

I seek out food up high in trees. I munch mostly on leaves.
I can see long distances from way up here, where I almost touch the clouds. I have been known to gallop at speeds up to 30 miles per hour.

H is for Hippopotamus:

Most of my friends call me Hippo and you can too. But don't get too close to me, especially in the rivers. Most of our time is spent in the water and we hold our breath for periods of five minutes at a time.

I is for Iguana:

My lizard-like skin is very rough. I feed on small bugs and insects. I am in the reptile family. We live in Southern Mexico, South and Central America. Most of us are green in color.

J is for Jaguar:

I am one of the fastest land animals and I have been clocked at speeds of up to 35 miles an hour. I am known for my unusual color patches on my fur of black and orange.

33

K is for Kangaroo:

You can't out jump me or out run me, as I bound across the Australian grasslands. I am called a boxing kangaroo when men set up matches with me and them. I have strong kicking back legs too.

L is forLlama:

I am sometimes the size of a small horse. My neck is high in the air and I have a bad spitting habit. So don't make me mad or get too close. Some of us can weigh as much as 400 pounds and for 5,000 years my ancestors were used as pack animals much like camels are today.

34

M is for Monkey:

Most of us live in trees. We swing on vines from branch to branch to get to where we are going faster. We are pretty noisy when danger is near or when we are disturbed.

N is for Nuthatch:

I spend much of my time climbing upside down on branches. I am not much bigger than a sparrow, but you will never see them standing on their heads.

35

O is for Octopus: So many arms and so little to do. My eight tentacles are usually mistaken for feet. Stay clear of my black poisonous spray that I use to scare off predators. Oh, and be careful handling us as we do bite and that is poisonous too. There is a rumor floating around that some of us have adapted to living in trees. It is just not so – after all I should know, I am one.

P is for Penguin: We live mostly in the Southern Hemisphere, such as South America, South Africa, Australia, and New Zealand. We mate in autumn so that our young will be born in more desirable weather. We eat primarily fish and try to stay clear of the leopard seals who want to eat us. We are safe from them on land, but we rarely stand a chance in open water where seals are lightning fast.

Q is for Quail:

Sometimes I'm called a ruffled grouse, because when I am scared I take off and loudly flap my wings. My feathers on my tail fan out widely also. We eat food off of the forest floor and we like to hide in trees. We live in groups call coveys and can have as many as 200 birds together.

R is for Rhinoceros:

You can call me rhino. As big as I am, I still can charge and run 35 miles an hour. We do not stay together in groups for long, but we tend to go our separate ways and so we are called a charge of rhinos.

S is for Seal:

I live in cold salt water and I eat fish all day. I am in water most of my life and I move faster in it than on dry land. I need to be quick to escape my enemies. I love to be the star of the show at the zoo and to entertain you with my fancy flippers. (It looks like I am clapping my hands.)

T is for Tiger:

My growl sounds bad enough, but my bite is much worse. Never get to close to my cage or stick your hands into it. I have black stripes on my body like the zebra does.

U is for Unicorn:

I look just like a horse, except for my one big horn. It protrudes from the center of my forehead. I am really make believe, but children love to hear about me in stories. It is fun and helps their imagination.

V is for Vampire Bat:

All night I fly around. For being blind I do just fine. I use my radar to keep me from bumping into things. Flying bugs and moths are such tasty treats for me.

W is for Whale:

I am the biggest of all fish. Some folks love to watch us swim. We try to stay way out in the ocean, but sometimes we get lost and end up beached on the shoreline and need the help of man.

X is for X- ray fish:

Have you ever seen a fish you could see right through it, that's me. We come in many colors and many people like to keep us in aquariums in their homes. A common name for us is tetra.

40

Y is for Yak:

I am odd looking yes I know. I have hair from the top of my head down my back and even on my joints and toes. I look like a small version of a water buffalo. I could really use a hair cut.

Z is for Zebra:

I look a lot like a horse, but just a little shorter. I look just like a jailbird with my fancy black striped coat. My native home is Africa, but you can visit me in your local zoos.

the Alphabet Zoo

So there you have it - the animals of the world. I hope we take good enough care of each of them and give them their space, their own place to live and play. We have lost some special animals for many reasons. Those creatures will not be coming back; they are lost forever. The good news is that there are hundreds, if not thousands of animal shelters and places where our endangered animals can go if they were ever in trouble.

Below is a collection of sites that I'm aware of where animal care is their business. Each of us can do are part too in keeping these special friends around a while longer. We can click on these links or go to these websites and help support our animal friends.

See all of the links below and let's go there right away and visit them. They really need our help. If we care enough about our

environment and world, we will make saving the animals one of our major goals in life. Consider doing book reports about animals too or share about your very own special pet friends living under your roof.

ANIMAL LINKS BEGIN HERE

http://www.lionaid.org

http://www.wildlife-rescue.org.uk

https://www.wildlife-rescue.org

https://www.facebook.com/CritterCamp

http://www.elephants.com

https://www.facebook.com/adltexas